T0368377

AND I WAS TOLD THAT HE, CHRIST JESUS, IS GOD ALSO

THE DIVINE TRUTH

BARBARA ANN MARY MACK

authorHOUSE

AuthorHouse™
1663 Liberty Drive
Bloomington, IN 47403
www.authorhouse.com
Phone: 833-262-8899

Published by AuthorHouse 10/17/2024

ISBN: 979-8-8230-3653-5 (sc)
ISBN: 979-8-8230-3655-9 (hc)
ISBN: 979-8-8230-3654-2 (e)

Library of Congress Control Number: 2024922179

Print information available on the last page.

This book is printed on acid-free paper.

BEHOLD MY PRESENT TESTAMENT, THE CONTINUANCE OF MY OLD AND NEW TESTAMENTS, SAYS THE LORD GOD

BY:

BARBARA ANN MARY MACK

BEGAN: AUGUST 10, 2024

COMPLETED: AUGUST 10, 2024

DEDICATION

TO THE FOREVER-LIVING GOD; CHRIST JESUS

ALLELUIA!!!

ACKNOWLEDGMENT

THE REALITY OF CHRIST JESUS' DIVINITY HAS ENTERED THE MINDS AND HEARTS OF EARTH'S BELIEVING RESIDENTS

HALLELUJAH!!!

ABOUT THE BOOK

AND I WAS TOLD THAT HE, CHRIST JESUS, IS GOD ALSO

REVEALS MY EXPERIENCE AS A CONVERTED CATHOLIC AND BELIEVER.

BEING RAISED IN A NON-CATHOLIC DENOMINATION, I DID NOT UNDERSTAND WHEN I WOULD HEAR CATHOLICS AND OTHER CHRISTIAN DENOMINATION MEMBERS SAY, OR REFER TO CHRIST JESUS AS GOD. BUT WHEN I CONVERTED TO THE CATHOLIC FAITH, AFTER LEAVING MY FORMER RELIGIOUS BELIEFS, I SOMEWHAT UNDERSTOOD WHAT THE OTHER CHRISTIAN FAITHS MEANT. PRIOR TO MY CONVERSION IN 1997, I BEGAN RECEIVING VISIONS IN REFERENCE TO SPIRITUAL ENLIGHTENMENTS FROM ALMIGHTY GOD. WHILE RECEIVING THE VISUAL AND SPIRITUAL ENLIGHTENMENTS, I NEVER QUESTIONED THE ORIGIN OR SOURCE. THINGS WERE REVEALED TO ME IN A WAY THAT I UNDERSTOOD OR KNEW THE MEANING AND PURPOSE OF THE REVELATIONS. MANY THINGS AND MESSAGES THAT I RECEIVED REFERRED TO JESUS CHRIST AS ALMIGHTY GOD, THE SON.

ABOUT THE AUTHOR

BARBARA IS A FORMER PSYCHOLOGY AND SOCIOLOGY STUDENT OF COMMUNITY COLLEGE OF PHILADELPHIA. BARBARA'S DESIRE AT THE TIME WAS TO BECOME A STRESS MANAGEMENT THERAPIST. BUT, BEFORE OBTAINING AN ASSOCIATE DEGREE IN SOCIOLOGY, BARBARA WAS SPIRITUALLY LED TO FOCUS ON THE CHRISTIAN FAITH, IN REGARDS TO WRITING DOWN WHAT APPEARED TO BE DICTATIONS FROM ALMIGHTY GOD. BARBARA BEGAN TRAVELING TO OTHER AREAS OF THE WORLD AND SHARING THE MESSAGES THAT SHE RECEIVED FROM GOD.

BARBARA TAKING DOWN DICTATION FROM ALMIGHTY GOD, THE FATHER

PROLOGUE

IN THE BEGINNING, LOVE, CHRIST JESUS, WAS CALLED INTO EXISTENCE BY ALMIGHTY GOD, HIS HEAVENLY ORIGIN AND DIVINE FATHER.

IN THE BEGINNING CHRIST JESUS MAINTAINED HIS POSITON AS ALMIGHTY GOD, THE DIVINE SON.

IN THE BEGINNING JEHOVAH GOD, THE FATHER, AND CHRIST JESUS, HIS ONLY BEGOTTEN SON, WERE UNITED IN EVERYTHING THAT WAS/IS HOLY AND ETERNAL.

IN THE BEGINNING, CHRIST JESUS BECAME GOD, THE FATHER'S, HEAVENLY WORD.

IN THE BEGINNING CHRIST JESUS AND GOD, HIS FATHER, LIVED IN SWEET HARMONY ABOVE THE UNIVERSE AND THE PLANET EARTH.

IN THE BEGINNING MANKIND WAS CALLED INTO EXISTENCE AND WAS FORMED IN A MANNER THAT PLEASED GOD, THE FATHER, AND CHRIST JESUS, HIS ONLY BEGOTTEN SON.

IN THE BEGINNING, CHRIST JESUS MOVED IN THE MIDST OF SWEET HEAVEN BY THE DIVINE POWER AND GRACE THAT FLOWED THROUGH AND FROM THE LIVING ESSENCE OF JEHOVAH GOD, THE FATHER. BECAUSE CHRIST JESUS WAS NOT CREATED LIKE MANKIND, BUT CAME FORTH FROM GOD, THE FATHER, HE TOO IS GOD. HE SHARES HIS FATHER'S DIVINITY, BECAUSE GOD, THE FATHER, BEGAT JESUS.

ALLELUIA!!!

INTRODUCTION

CHRIST JESUS, GOD, THE FATHER'S, LIVING WORD, BECAME HUMAN AND LIVED AMONG THE WORTHY ONES NOT SO LONG AGO. HE WAS SENT BY GOD, HIS HEAVENLY FATHER, TO REVEAL EVERYTHING THAT HIS FATHER TOLD HIM TO CONVEY. ALTHOUGH JESUS MAINTAINED HIS DIVINITY, HE BECAME A NATURAL HUMAN BEING IN ORDER TO SHARE IN MANKIND'S ABILITIES AND INABILITIES. HE ENTERED THIS WORLD IN THE FORM OF A REAL HUMAN BABY. HE WENT THROUGH THE CUSTOMS THAT WERE PRACTICED BY THE JEWISH COMMUNITY AT THAT TIME. ALTHOUGH ALMIGHTY GOD, THE FATHER, IS JESUS' ORIGIN, GOD APPOINTED HIM A SURROGATE EARTHLY FATHER NAMED JOSEPH. GOD ALSO CHOSE AND APPOINTED MARY AS JESUS' EARTHLY MOTHER.

CHAPTER ONE

I AM WHO I AM, SAYS THE LORD JESUS

THE LORD JESUS SPEAKING TO EARTH'S RESIDENTS TODAY

I AM WHO I AM, **SAYS THE LORD JESUS.**
I HAVE COME TO REVEAL MY HEAVENLY FATHER'S HOLY PRESENCE AND WORDS TO EVERYONE; **INCLUDING THE RIGHTEOUS.**

I AM YOUR LORD; AND **I AM YOUR GOD.**
I AM HE WHO DESCENDED FROM MY FATHER'S REALM OF **HEAVEN SENT DIVINE LOVE.**

REMEMBER THIS **TRUTH, DEAR CHILDREN-**
FOR, TO DENY ME AS GOD, IS **TRULY AN ABOMINATION.**

REMEMBER WHAT **I TELL YOU-**
FOR, MY WORDS ARE **HOLY, ETERNAL, AND TRUE.**

I CAME FROM THE LIVING AND **ETERNAL BEING-**
OF GOD, THE **FATHER, AND KING.**

THEREFORE, **DEAR ONE-**
I AM HIS ONLY **BEGOTTEN LIVING SON.**

FOR, JEHOVAH **GOD, YOU SEE-**
CALLED INTO EXISTENCE, THE HOLY BEING THAT
CAME FORTH FROM **HOLY ETERNAL HE.**

JEHOVAH GOD, **THE ALMIGHTY-**
CALLED INTO EXISTENCE **BLESSED ME.**

HOLY, HOLY, HOLY-
IS THE ESSENCE OF JEHOVAH GOD ALMIGHTY!!!

DEAR CHILDREN, **CAN YOU NOT SEE-**
THAT I AM THE ONLY BEGOTTEN SON OF **JEHOVAH**
GOD, THE ALMIGHTY.

LISTEN, LISTEN, LISTEN-
LISTEN TO WHAT I HAVE TO SAY, O DECEIVED AND
HARD HEARTED NATION.

FOR, I AM **INDEED, YOU SEE-**
THE GODLY PRODUCT OF **THE FATHER ALMIGHTY.**

I CAN PERFORM MIRACLES LIKE MY HEAVENLY **GOD**
AND FATHER.
ONLY ME, AND **NO OTHER.**

FOR, **I ALONE, YOU SEE-**
CAME FORTH FROM THE HOLY BEING OF **MY**
HEAVENLY FATHER ALMIGHTY.

Barbara Ann Mary Mack

FOR, **HOLY**, YOU SEE-
IS THE GOD AND FATHER WHO CHOSE TO BRING INTO
EXISTENCE **HOLY ME.**

LOOK UPON ME, O **NON-BELIEVING ONE-**
FOR, I AM JEHOVAH GOD'S **ONLY BEGOTTEN SON!!!**

GAZE UPON ME-
GAZE UPON THE ONLY BEGOTTEN SON; **CHRIST
JESUS, THE ALMIGHTY.**

FOR, AS GOD, THE SON, **I DO EXIST.**
BEHOLD, O UNBELIEVING ONES, I NOW WALK **IN YOUR
BLESSED MIDST.**

BEHOLD MY **HOLY EXISTENCE-**
LOOK UPON MY **VISIBLE PRESENCE.**

CAN YOU **NOT SEE-**
THE DIVINE BEAUTY THAT **SURROUNDS HOLY ME?**

IT MAY BE HARD FOR YOU **TO UNDERSTAND-**
THAT I CAME FORTH BY THE POWER OF **ALMIGHTY
GOD'S HOLY HAND.**

HOLY, HOLY, HOLY-
IS THE ONLY BEGOTTEN SON OF GOD, THE FATHER,
ALMIGHTY!!!**

BELIEVE IN ME-
BELIEVE IN GOD, **THE FATHER, ALMIGHTY.**

BELIEVE IN THE **HEAVEN SENT HOLY ONE.**
BELIEVE IN GOD, THE FATHER'S, **ONLY BEGOTTEN SON.**

FOR, I AM HOLY, AND **I AM TRUE-**
I AM THE HOLY ONE WHO **SAVES BLESSED YOU.**

FOR, HE **CHOSE, YOU SEE-**
TO CALL INTO EXISTENCE **HOLY ETERNAL ME.**

I AM **THE REAL THING-**
I AM CHRIST JESUS; GOD, THE FATHER'S, BLESSED
SON, **AND HEAVENLY KING.**

I CAN DO EVERYTHING THAT THE FATHER **PERMITS,**
YOU SEE-
BECAUSE I AM ALSO GOD, **THE FOREVER LIVING
ALMIGHTY.**

HOLY, HOLY, HOLY, YOU SEE-
IS THE ONLY BEGOTTEN SON OF JEHOVAH GOD
ALMIGHTY!!!

I HAVE WATCHED OVER THE BLESSED ONES WHO
BELONG TO ME-
AND I HAVE DEFEATED SATAN, **OUR ENEMY.**

Barbara Ann Mary Mack

CHRIST JESUS SPEAKING TO ALMIGHTY GOD, HIS HEAVENLY FATHER

I THANK YOU, MY HOLY **GOD AND FATHER-**
FOR GIVING ME AUTHORITY OVER YOUR EARTHLY
NEEDY **SON AND DAUGHTER.**

FOR, **TRULY-**
THEY NEED THE CARE OF YOU AND YOUR ONLY
BEGOTTEN SON; **CHRIST JESUS, THE ALMIGHTY.**

FOR, **YOU AND I-**
WILL LEAD THEM AWAY FROM THE REALM OF
DESTRUCTION, SO THAT **THEIR BLESSED SOULS WILL
NOT SPIRITUALLY DIE.**

HOLY, HOLY, HOLY-
IS MY FATHER GOD ALMIGHTY!!!

FOR, HE **TEACHES ME-**
THE GOOD THAT COMES WITH KNOWING **SWEET
ETERNITY (ALMIGHTY GOD).**

I BLESS YOU, **DEAR FATHER-**
FOR SHARING YOUR HOLY PRESENCE WITH MY
HUMAN **EARTHLY SISTER AND BROTHER.**

FOR, **THEY TOO-**

ARE WORTHY TO KNOW AND **LOVE BLESSING YOU.**

THEY TOO-
DESERVE TO WITNESS THE MERCY AND GRACE THAT **COME FROM HOLY YOU.**

THEY TOO-
DESERVE TO BEHOLD THE POWER THAT **COMES FROM YOU.**

THEY TOO, YOU SEE-
DESERVE TO BEHOLD THE ONLY BEGOTTEN SON OF THE FOREVER LIVING **GOD AND FATHER ALMIGHTY.**

FOR, **HOLY, YOU SEE-**
IS THE ONLY BEGOTTEN SON CALLED **CHRIST JESUS, THE ALMIGHTY.**

FOR, **HOLY, YOU SEE-**
IS THE SON OF **GOD ALMIGHTY.**

FOR, EVERY DAY, **YOU SEE-**
I SIT ON THE THRONE THAT IS NEXT TO **GOD, THE FATHER, ALMIGHTY.**

HOLY, HOLY, HOLY-
IS THE ETERNAL LIVING THRONE OF JEHOVAH GOD, **THE ALMIGHTY!!!**

Barbara Ann Mary Mack

I WILL SIT ON THE MIGHTY THRONE **NEXT TO MY FATHER-**
I WILL SIT ON MY HOLY THRONE AS I WATCH **HEAVEN'S SWEET REJOICING RESIDENTS GATHER.**

FOR, THEY GATHER, **YOU SEE-**
AROUND THE HOLY THRONE OF **GOD ALMIGHTY.**

HOLY, HOLY, HOLY-
IS GOD, MY LIVING FATHER, THE ALMIGHTY.

I WILL TEACH MY EARTHLY SIBLINGS ABOUT YOU, DEAR FATHER

CHRIST JESUS SPEAKING TO ALMIGHTY GOD, HIS HEAVENLY FATHER

I WILL TEACH THEM, **DEAR FATHER-**
THAT THEY MUST LOVE AND **TRUST EACH OTHER.**

I WILL TEACH THEM **TO LOVE-**
OUR HEAVENLY **GOD AND FATHER ABOVE.**

FOR, **HOLY AND TRUE-**
IS THE LOVE THAT THE BELIEVING ONES AND I HAVE FOR **ETERNAL YOU.**

HOLY, HOLY, HOLY-

IS OUR LOVE FOR GOD ALMIGHTY!!!

I WILL TEACH YOUR EARTHLY OFFSPRING **YOUR VERSION OF DIVINE LOVE.**
I WILL TEACH THEM THE HOLY TRUTH ABOUT **OUR HEAVENLY GOD AND FATHER ABOVE.**

I WILL TEACH THEM YOUR HOLY **UNCHANGING WORD-** AS I REVEAL TO THEM THINGS THAT **NO HUMAN BEING HAS HEARD.**

I WILL TEACH **THE TRUTH-**
THAT YOU HAVE SHARED WITH YOUR SENT PROPHETS AND MESSENGERS **FROM THEIR BLESSED YOU.**

I WILL TEACH THEM **EVERYTHING-**
ABOUT THEIR SOVEREIGN HEAVENLY GOD AND **DEVOTED KING.**

I WILL TEACH, I WILL TEACH-
I WILL TEACH YOUR EARTHLY LOVED ONES ABOUT THE HEAVENLY GOD AND FATHER **WHOM THEY CAN EASILY REACH.**

DEAR FATHER: LET YOU AND I GO DOWN AND SEE WHAT'S GOING ON WITH MY VULNERABLE EARTHLY SISTER AND BROTHER

THE LORD JESUS SPEAKING TO ALMIGHTY GOD, OUR FATHER

DEAR FATHER:
LET YOU AND I GO DOWN AND SEE WHAT IS HAPPENING WITH YOUR VULNERABLE SON AND DAUGHTER.

I CAN HEAR THEIR CRIES, YOU SEE.
FOR, THEY ARE BEING TORMENTED AND TORTURED BY SATAN, OUR ENEMY.

LET US GO DOWN AND SEE-
THE NEEDY OFFSPRING OF GOD ALMIGHTY.

FOR, I CAN TRULY HEAR-
THE CRIES OF OUR CHILDREN, FOR THEY ARE VERY NEAR.

I CAN SEE THEIR WEEPING FACES-
I CAN SEE THEM IN ALL OF EARTH'S HIDING PLACES.

I CAN SEE THEIR FALLING TEARS-
AS THEY WEPT THROUGH THE YEARS.

I CAN SEE THEIR JOYLESS SMILE-
AS THEY SLUMBER FOR A LITTLE WHILE.

LET US-

HELP THE SUFFERING SIBLINGS OF THE FOREVER
LIVING CHRIST JESUS-

FOR, THEY ARE YOURS AND MINE-
LET US HELP THEM, DEAR FATHER GOD, DURING
THIS SUFFERING PERIOD OF TIME.

LET US SEE-
THE HANDIWORK OF SATAN, OUR ENEMY.

FOR, HIS VISIBILITY-
CAUSES TREMENDOUS PAIN AND SUFFERING
TOWARD THE GREAT CREATION OF GOD ALMIGHTY.

CAN YOU HEAR THEIR CONTINUOUS CRIES, DEAR
FATHER?
CAN YOU HEAR THEIR TEARS AS THEY FALL FROM
THE EYES OF YOUR HURTING SON AND DAUGHTER?

DEAR FATHER GOD: WHAT CAN YOU AND I DO?
HOW CAN WE SEE THEM THROUGH?

FOR, THEY ARE WEEPING-
IN THE HOLY PRESENCE OF CHRIST JESUS, THEIR
HEAVENLY AND EARTHLY KING.

LET US SEE-

Barbara Ann Mary Mack

WHAT SATAN HAS DONE TO THE CHILDREN WHO NEED YOU AND ME.

LET US-
GO DOWN TO OUR LOVED ONES, SO THAT THEY MAY BE A WITNESS TO THE HOLY POWER OF YOUR BELOVED **SON; CHRIST JESUS.**

DEAR FATHER: LET US GO DOWN **TO EARTH'S NEEDY-** SO THAT THEY MAY FEEL THE UNLIMITED **POWER OF JEHOVAH GOD ALMIGHTY.**

LET THEM **BEHOLD-**
A HOLY GOD WHO IS MORE VALUABLE THAN **EVERY POT OF PURE UNSTAINED GOLD.**
DEAR FATHER GOD: LET EARTH'S NEEDY ONES BE A LIVING WITNESS, SAYS THE LORD JESUS

CHRIST JESUS SPEAKING TO ALMIGHTY GOD, HIS HEAVENLY FATHER.

O HOLY FATHER GOD: LET EARTH'S SPIRITUAL NEEDY ONES **BE A WITNESS-**
TO YOUR REALM OF DIVINE **LOVE AND KINDNESS.**

LET THEM BE **A WITNESS-**
TO YOUR REALM OF **UNENDING HOLINESS.**

FOR, **HOLY AND TRUE**-
IS THE GOODNESS AND MERCY THAT COME FROM
ETERNAL, **LOVING, AND ALMIGHTY** YOU.

LET US GO DOWN TO NEEDY **EARTH, DEAR FATHER**-
LET YOU AND I BE A WITNESS TO THE SUFFERING OF
OUR EARTHLY SON AND DAUGHTER.

LET US **FEEL**-
THE SUFFERING THAT IS **CONTINUOUS AND REAL.**

LET YOU AND I **BEHOLD**-
THE TEARS THAT **DO UNFOLD.**

LET US GO-
SO THAT **WE WILL KNOW.**

FOR, THEY ARE IN **NEED, YOU SEE**-
OF THE DIVINE HELP THAT COMES FROM **THE
ALMIGHTY.**

**NOW THAT YOU AND I HAVE DESCENDED FROM
HEAVEN'S OPEN GATE, SAYS THE LORD JESUS**

**THE LORD JESUS SPEAKING TO ALMIGHTY GOD, THE
FATHER**

NOW THAT YOU AND I HAVE DESCENDED FROM
SWEET HEAVEN'S OPEN GATE-
OUR SUFFERING CHILDREN WILL NO LONGER HAVE
TO WAIT.

FOR, SOME MAY BE ABLE TO SEE-
THE HOLY ESSENCE AND PRESENCE OF GOD, THE
FATHER, AND HIS ONLY BEGOTTEN SON ALMIGHTY.

FOR, I CAN SEE, I CAN SEE-
I CAN SEE THE SUFFERING CHILDREN OF GOD
ALMIGHTY.

I CAN HEAR THE CRIES THAT COME FROM THE
CHILDREN-
YES, THE CHILDREN OF EVERY NATION.

I CAN HEAR THEIR TREMBLING VOICE-
FOR, THEY NO LONGER HAVE THE STRENGTH TO
REJOICE.

LOOK OVER THERE, DEAR FATHER.
CAN YOU SEE THE TEARS THAT FOLLOW MY
SUFFERING EARTHLY BROTHER?

CAN YOU HEAR? CAN YOU HEAR?
CAN YOU HEAR MY BROTHER'S FALLING TEAR?

FOR, IT MAKES SUCH A **VERY LOUD SOUND**-
SO THAT YOU AND I WILL KNOW THAT **THE SUFFERING
ONES ARE AROUND.**

CAN YOU SEE THEIR FALLING **TEARS, DEAR GOD?**
CAN YOU SEE THEIR **FACELESS LOVE?**

THEIR FACES CANNOT BE **SEEN, YOU SEE**-
FOR, THEY HAVE LOST THEIR SMILING FACES TO
SATAN, OUR ENEMY.

CAN WE HELP THEM, **DEAR FATHER?**
CAN YOU AND I ASSIST MY **WORTHY SISTER AND
BROTHER?**
FOR, THEY **DESERVE, YOU SEE**-
THE HELP THAT COULD ONLY COME FROM GOD,
THE FATHER, AND **THE FOREVER LIVING CHRIST,
ALMIGHTY.**

DEAR FATHER GOD: LET US HELP **OUR SUFFERING
CHILDREN.**
LET US HELP **THIS HURTING NATION.**

WE CAN **DO IT**-
BY THE POWER OF **YOUR HOLY ETERNAL SPIRIT.**

YOU CAN DO IT, **DEAR FATHER GOD.**
YOU CAN DO IT BY THE POWER OF **YOUR DIVINE LOVE.**

FOR, **HOLY, YOU SEE-**
IS THE MIGHTY POWER OF SWEET **UNENDING ETERNITY (ALMIGHTY GOD).**

DEAR FATHER GOD: **LET US DO IT TODAY.**
LET YOU AND I HELP THEM **AS THEY PRAY.**

FOR, THEY WALK **THE BARREN STREET-**
BUT DO NOT HAVE THE STRENGTH TO SPEAK TO THOSE **WHOM THEY MEET.**

LET US GO TO THEM, AND GIVE THEM **A TASTE OF YOUR DIVINITY.**
LET THEM FEEL THE HOLY PRESENCE OF THEIR GREAT AND **HOLY GOD ALMIGHTY.**

FOR, YOU ARE GOOD AND HOLY, **DEAR FATHER OF MINE.**
AND, YOUR CHILDREN AND I WILL TREASURE YOUR HOLY PRESENCE **UNTIL THE END OF UNENDING TIME.**

HOLY, HOLY, HOLY-
IS THE GOODNESS OF MY GOD AND FATHER ALMIGHTY!!!

DEAR FATHER GOD: LET THEM SEE YOU, SAYS THE LORD JESUS

THE LORD JESUS SPEAKING TO GOD, THE FATHER

LET THEM **SEE YOU**-
LET THE CHILDREN SEE THE HOLY PRESENCE OF
THEIR **GOD; SWEET INFINITY.**

FOR, **HOLY AND REAL**-
IS THE HEAVEN SENT PRESENCE THAT THE BLESSED
ONES CAN **TRULY SEE AND FEEL.**

O HOLY GOD AND **ETERNAL FATHER**-
LET US HELP YOUR LOVED ONES **AS THEY GATHER.**

FOR, **HOLY AND TRUE**-
IS THE REALM OF UNENDING LOVE THAT **COMES
FROM BLESSED YOU.**

HOLY ARE YOU, **DEAR FATHER.**
HOLY IS THE LOVE THAT YOU SHARE WITH MY NEEDY
EARTHLY SISTER AND BROTHER.

YOU ARE THE **DIVINE PURE ONE**-
WHO BEGAT ME, **YOUR ONLY DIVINE SON.**

I ADORE YOU, **DEAR FATHER GOD**-
AND I WILL ALWAYS TREASURE YOUR REALM **OF
UNENDING LOVE.**

Barbara Ann Mary Mack

MY DEVOTION-
IS TO MY HEAVENLY FATHER AND **HIS GREAT CREATION.**

COME, **DEAR FATHER-**
LET YOU AND I OFFER YOUR REALM OF DIVINE LOVE
TO **MY HURTING SISTER AND BROTHER.**

LET THEM **TASTE AND SEE-**
YOUR DIVINE **POWER AND MAJESTY.**

COME, **O SOVEREIGN ONE!**
JOIN THE TEARS OF YOUR EARTHLY LOVED ONES
AND **YOUR ONLY BEGOTTEN SON.**

COME, O SWEET REALM OF **UNENDING DIVINITY.**
JOIN LIFE-SAVING **HOLY ME.**

LET US GO AND **JOIN OUR LOVED ONES-**
DEAR FATHER GOD: LET US JOIN OUR HURTING WELL-
LOVED **DAUGHTERS AND SONS.**

I CAN SEE THEM WALKING DOWN THE LONELY ROAD
AND ABANDON HIGHWAYS **OVER THERE.**
COME, DEAR FATHER: LET US SHOW THEM THAT **WE DO CARE.**

ALMIGHTY GOD; THE LORD JESUS, SPEAKING TO HIS EARTHLY CHILDREN TODAY

DEAR CHILDREN-
O, NEEDY ONES FROM **EVERY BLESSED NATION.**

MY FATHER AND I HAVE **COME TO HELP YOU.**
LET US HELP THE CHILDREN OF THE GOD WHO IS **HOLY, ETERNAL AND TRUE.**

COME, DEAR BROTHER!
RECEIVE THE LOVE AND HELP FROM **YOUR DEVOTED ORIGIN AND FATHER.**

COME OVER HERE, **DEAR SISTER OF MINE.**
JOIN THE GOD AND FATHER WHO IS **ONE OF A KIND.**

COME, DEAR ONE-
YOU ARE IN THE HOLY PRESENCE OF GOD, THE FATHER'S, **ONLY BEGOTTEN SON.**

FOR, WE HAVE COME TO **HELP YOU TODAY.**
WE HAVE COME, SO THAT WE MAY LEAD YOU TO **MY LIFE REWARDING HOLY WAY.**

COME WITH US-
SO THAT YOU MAY EXPERIENCE **THE DIVINITY OF CHRIST JESUS-**

Barbara Ann Mary Mack

FOR, I AM **YOUR HEAVENLY BROTHER.**

I HAVE COME TO BACK TO EARTH WITH **GOD, OUR HOLY ETERNAL FATHER.**

LET THE HOLY CHURCH BELLS RING

CHRIST JESUS, THE LORD GOD, SPEAKING TODAY

RING, O MIGHTY CHURCH BELLS, RING!
FOR, YOU ARE IN THE HOLY PRESENCE OF CHRIST JESUS, **YOUR EARTHLY AND HEAVENLY KING!**

LET THE CHURCH BELLS RING!
LET THEM SOUND LOUD IN THE HOLY PRESENCE OF **CHRIST JESUS; THE DIVINE GOD AND KING!**

LET THEM RING-
FOR, I, THE LORD JESUS, HAVE COME TO DO **A GREAT AND WONDERFUL THING.**

RING! RING! RING!
RING, O PRECIOUS BELLS OF THE **ALMIGHTY GOD, AND KING!**

RING, O BLESSED **BELLS, RING!**
RING, AS YOU SALUTE CHRIST JESUS, EARTH'S AND **HEAVEN'S MIGHTY SENT KING!**

RING **LOUD AND CLEAR-**
SO THAT EARTH'S NEEDY RESIDENTS WILL KNOW
THAT I **AM VERY NEAR!**

FOR, I HAVE **COME, YOU SEE-**
WITH THE HOLY SPIRIT OF **GOD, THE FATHER,
ALMIGHTY.**

REJOICE! REJOICE! REJOICE!!!

THE LORD JESUS SPEAKING TO EARTH'S NEEDY ONES TODAY

REJOICE, **EVERY LAND!**
GIVE PRAISE TO OUR GOD AND FATHER, FOR HE
HOLDS YOU ALL IN **THE POWER OF HIS HOLY HAND!**

GIVE HIM **CONTINUOUS PRAISE-**
THROUGHOUT THESE **BLESSED DAYS.**

FOR, HE IS **GOOD, YOU SEE-**
TO HIS EARTHLY **CHILDREN AND ME.**

HOLY, HOLY, HOLY-
IS MY FATHER, GOD ALMIGHTY!!!

REJOICE, **O WAKEN LAND!**
GIVE PRAISE TO GOD'S **LIFE GIVING HAND!**

Barbara Ann Mary Mack

FOR, **HE IS TRUE-**
HE IS THE KING AND GOD OVER ME AND **BLESSED YOU.**

RING, AND SING! RING, AND SING!
RING AND SING IN THE HOLY PRESENCE OF **JEHOVAH GOD, THE MIGHTY HEAVENLY KING!**

REJOICE! REJOICE! REJOICE!!!
SHOW YOUR GRATITUDE AS YOU SING IN ONE **UNIFIED HEAVEN BOUND VOICE!**

FOR, **GOD, THE ALMIGHTY-**
HAS DESCENDED FROM SWEET HEAVEN IN THE MIDST OF **HIS UNENDING DIVINITY.**

HOLY, HOLY, HOLY-
IS MY GRACIOUS GOD AND **FATHER ALMIGHTY!!!**

FOR, **I AM GLAD-**
THAT MY EARTHLY BROTHERS AND SISTERS ARE NO LONGER **HURTING AND SAD.**

FOR, ALMIGHTY **GOD AND ME-**
HAVE COME TO SHARE OUR REALM OF **SWEET UNENDING DIVINITY.**

I AM FULL OF **DIVINE JOY-**

AS MY HOLY FATHER GREETS EVERY LITTLE **GIRL AND BOY.**

FOR, **HOLY AND TRUE-**
IS THE GOD WHO **RESCUED YOU.**

DEAR HEAVENLY FATHER AND GOD: SHALL WE STAY DOWN HERE FOR AWHILE?

THE LORD JESUS SPEAKING TO GOD, THE FATHER

SHALL WE; SHALL WE? SHALL YOU AND I STAY DOWN HERE **FOR A WHILE?**
SHALL YOU AND I SHOW EARTH'S RESIDENT OUR UNIQUE PRESENCE AND **DIVINE STYLE?**

SHALL WE STAY HERE ON EARTH **FOR A LITTLE WHILE?**
LET US STAY, DEAR FATHER, UNTIL WE SEE YOUR LOVED ONES **HEAVEN SENT SMILE.**

LET US SIT-
AS WE SHARE **YOUR HOLY SPIRIT.**

FOR, OUR LOVED **ONES NEED-**
THE GOD AND FATHER WHO DOES **CARE AND FEED.**

LET US STAY-

UNTIL THE END OF **THE NEW DAY.**

ALMIGHTY GOD, THE FATHER, SPEAKING TO CHRIST JESUS, HIS ONLY BEGOTTEN DIVINE SON

WE WILL **SIT, MY SON-**
FOR, OUR **BATTLE IS WON.**

WE WILL SIT **FOR AWHILE-**
UNTIL YOU AND I SEE MY **SWEET CHILDREN SMILE.**

COME, **MY HOLY SON.**
LET YOU AND I SIT; FOR **WE HAVE WON.**

SATAN, OUR **ENEMY, YOU SEE-**
CANNOT DESTROY THE CHILDREN WHO BELONG TO
HOLY UNENDING ME.

LET US **RELAX FOR AWHILE-**
UNTIL YOU AND I WITNESS **THEIR LONGED FOR SMILE.**

PURE DIVINE LOVE

THE LORD JESUS SPEAKING TO ALMIGHTY GOD, HIS HEAVENLY FATHER

DEAR FATHER GOD: LET YOU AND I EXHIBIT **PURE DIVINE LOVE.**

SO THAT OUR EARTHLY LOVED ONES WILL
EXPERIENCE THE GLORY THAT **DESCENDED WITH
US FROM SWEET HEAVEN ABOVE.**

LET THEM SEE-
THE DEPTH OF **YOUR MAJESTY.**

LET THEM **BEHOLD AND WITNESS-**
YOUR **SPIRITUAL VASTNESS.**

FOR, **HOLY, YOU SEE-**
IS MY FATHER AND **GOD ALMIGHTY.**

LET YOUR **DIVINE LOVE PERMEATE-**
YOUR OPEN **HEAVENLY GATE.**

FOR, **HOLY AND TRUE-**
IS THE HEAVENLY GATE THAT WAS **OPENED BY YOU.**

COME, DEAR FATHER-
LET US JOIN BARBARA, OUR OBEDIENT **EARTHLY
DAUGHTER.**

LET HER **WITNESS-**
YOUR SPIRITUAL **VASTNESS.**

LET HER **SEE-**
YOUR DIVINE **BEAUTY.**

THE LORD JESUS SPEAKING TO BARBARA

COME, DEAR BARBARA.
SIT FOR AWHILE, WITH ALMIGHTY GOD, OUR
HEAVENLY **ORIGIN AND FATHER.**

FOR, HE WANTS **YOU TO SEE-**
THE DEPTHS OF **HIS DIVINITY.**

HE WANTS **YOU TO KNOW-**
THAT HIS HOLY SPIRIT AND PRESENCE ARE WITH
YOU **WHEREVER YOU GO.**

DEAR BARBARA: **SIT WITH US-**
SIT WITH OUR HEAVENLY GOD AND FATHER; AND
YOUR LOVING **BROTHER CHRIST JESUS.**

FOR, **HOLY AND TRUE-**
IS GOD, THE FATHER, WHO HAS CONTINUOUS **LOVE
FOR ME AND YOU.**

HOLY, HOLY, HOLY-
IS THE REALM CALLED **GOD ALMIGHTY!!!**

HE IS FAITHFUL, AND **HE IS DIVINE TRUTH.**
HE HAS BEEN WITH YOU, DEAR BARBARA, SINCE
BEFORE YOUR PHYSICAL **EXISTENCE AND YOUR
BLESSED YOUTH.**

HOLY, HOLY, HOLY-
ARE, GOD, THE FATHER, YOU, AND ME; CHRIST JESUS,
THE ALMIGHTY!!!

HOLY, HOLY, HOLY-
IS OUR BLESSED ORIGIN; GOD, THE FATHER,
ALMIGHTY!!!

WHEN GOD, THE FATHER, AND I, LEAVE EARTH
TODAY, SAYS THE LORD JESUS

THE LORD JESUS SPEAKING

WHEN GOD, OUR HEAVENLY FATHER, AND I; LEAVE
EARTH'S REALM TODAY-
WE WILL REMAIN WITH EARTH'S RESIDENTS WHEN
YOU REJOICE AND PRAY.

WE WILL BE WITH YOU ALL WHENEVER YOU PRAY
TO GOD, THE FATHER-
WE WILL BE WITH OUR EARTHLY NEEDY SON AND
DAUGHTER.

WE WILL STAY-
LONG ENOUGH TO HEAR YOU ALL SING AND PRAY.

REJOICE, DEAR DAUGHTER!

Barbara Ann Mary Mack

REJOICE WITH CHRIST JESUS, AND **JEHOVAH GOD, THE FATHER!**

REJOICE! REJOICE! REJOICE!!!
LIFT UP YOUR SWEET AND **PRECIOUS UNITED VOICE!**

FOR, I WILL NEVER **LEAVE YOU ALL.**
I AM VERY NEAR, JUST **WHISPER YOUR HOLY CALL.**

I WILL HEAR-
THE VOICE OF MY DAUGHTER, **WHO DOES CARE.**

FOR, **HOLY AND TRUE-**
IS THE FATHER WHO IS ALWAYS NEAR **BELOVED YOU.**

HOLY, HOLY, HOLY,
IS THE BLESSED DAUGHTER AND MESSENGER OF GOD ALMIGHTY!!!

THE LORD JESUS SPEAKING TO BARBARA

I AM DIVINE **TRUTH, DEAR BARBARA.**
I WILL NEVER **FORSAKE YOU FOR ANOTHER.**

I AM REAL! I AM REAL!
LOOK AT ME, DEAR BARBARA, FOR I AM THE HOLY ESSENCE THAT **YOUR BLESSED SOUL CAN TRULY SEE AND FEEL.**

HOLY, HOLY, HOLY-
IS THE BLESSED FATHER ALMIGHTY!!!

THE REALM OF HOLINESS HAS DEPARTED FROM
EARTH'S BARREN LAND.

GOD, THE FATHER, SPEAKING

THE REALM OF HOLINESS HAS PARTED FROM
EARTH'S BARREN LAND-
AND NOW, MY ONLY BEGOTTEN SON; CHRIST JESUS,
AND I, HAVE LEFT EARTH'S RESIDENTS WITH A
DIVINE LOVE THAT THEY WILL FOREVER RESPECT
AND UNDERSTAND.

HOLY, HOLY, HOLY-
IS THE EARTHLY DEPARTURE OF GOD ALMIGHTY!!!

ALLELUIA! ALLELUIA! ALLELUIA!!!

BOOK TWO

AND WHEN ALMIGHTY GOD
ENTERED THE CHURCH

SUBTITLE:
WHAT WILL YOU DO?

BY

BARBARA ANN MARY MACK

BEHOLD MY PRESENT TESTAMENT, SAYS THE LORD JESUS AND WHEN ALMIGHTY GOD ENTERED THE CHURCH

SUBTITLE:
WHAT WILL YOU DO?

BY

BARBARA ANN MARY MACK

BEGAN: OCTOBER 12, 2024 –
COMPLETED: OCTOBER 12, 2024

DEDICATION

TO THE INFINITE CHRIST JESUS AND HIS FAITHFUL
AND REPENTANT CLERGY TODAY

ACKNOWLEDGMENT

THE REALITY AND VISIBILITY OF CHRIST JESUS' HOLY PRESENCE IN OUR BLESSED MIDST TODAY, IS MANIFESTED THROUGH THE GOD DICTATED WRITINGS THAT FLOW THROUGH BARBARA ANN MARY MACK'S HOLY PUBLISHED BOOKS TODAY.

I GIVE ALMIGHTY GOD CONTINUOUS PRAISE! FOR HE HAS FOUND THIS GENERATION WORTHY TO RECEIVE HIS LIFE SAVING MESSAGES TODAY.

HOLY IS HIS PERFECT NAME AND VISIBLE PRESENCE

HALLELUJAH!!!

BARBARA ANN MARY MACK

CHAPTER ONE

AND WHEN ALMIGHTY GOD ENTERED THE CHURCH

<u>ALMIGHTY GOD SPEAKING TO EARTH'S RESIDENTS TODAY</u>

WHY? WHY? **WHY?**
WHY DO YOU **TRY TO DENY?**

WHY DO YOU SUGARCOAT **THE TRUTH-**
THAT WAS REVEALED TO YOU **IN YOUR BLESSED YOUTH?**

WHY DO YOU **PASTORS AND CLERGY-**
DENY AND HIDE WHAT WAS REVEALED TO YOU BY
GOD ALMIGHTY?

HAVE YOU **NO SHAME-**
AS YOU UTTER AND SPEAK **MY HOLY NAME?**

DO YOU **NOT FEAR-**
THE HOLY GOD WHO IS **VERY NEAR?**

DO YOU NOT **HUMBLE, YOU SEE-**
YOUR PRESENCE THAT IS **VISIBLE TO ME?**

WHAT SHOULD **I DO**-
AS YOU BLASPHEME THE HOLY PRESENCE OF THE
ONLY GOD WHO IS **ETERNAL AND TRUE?**

WHAT SHOULD I DO TO **THE UNFAITHFUL CLERGY?**
WHAT SHOULD I DO TO THE LEADERS OF THE
CHURCH WHO DO NOT GIVE **HONOR TO THE CREATOR
ALMIGHTY?**

WHAT? WHAT? WHAT DO YOU PROFESSED CHURCH
LEADERS BELIEVE THAT **I SHOULD DO**-
TO THOSE WHOM I PLACED IN CHARGE OF THE
MESSAGES THAT ARE **HEAVEN SENT AND TRUE?**

WHAT? WHAT? **WHAT DO YOU SEE FIT**-
AS A PUNISHMENT FOR THOSE WHO **DISRESPECT MY
HOLY SPIRIT?**

I AM LISTENING-
TO THE CLERGY WHO CONTINUOUSLY DISRESPECT
THE HOLINESS OF **CHRIST JESUS, YOUR ETERNAL
GOD AND KING.**

I AM **WAITING**-
ANSWER ME, BEFORE I MAKE **YOUR PUNISHMENT
EVERLASTING.**

ANSWER! ANSWER! ANSWER-

YOUR DISPLEASED **HOLY GOD AND CREATOR!**

RESPOND TO ME BEFORE **IT IS TOO LATE.**
ANSWER MY REQUEST BEFORE I **CLOSE HEAVEN'S SWEET OPEN GATE.**

FOR, YOU ARE RUNNING OUT OF **VALUABLE TIME, DEAR ONES.**
I HAVE PLACED YOU OVER MY VULNERABLE **DAUGHTERS AND SONS.**

WHAT WILL **YOU DO TODAY?**
WILL YOU REPENT AND **FOLLOW MY HOLY WAY?**

WILL YOU LEAD MY WORTHY **UNSUSPECTED CHILDREN-**
TO MY HOLY **INSEPARABLE PURE NATION?**

WHAT? WHAT? WHAT WILL **YOU ALL DO?**
WILL YOU TELL MY TRUTH AS YOU PREACH TO **THE CALLED AND CHOSEN FEW?**

WILL YOU **REPENT?**
WILL YOU GIVE HONOR AND RESPECT TO THE MESSENGERS WHOM **I HAVE SENT?**

WHAT WILL YOU DO, O CLERGY?

WILL YOU REFORM AND REPENT IN THE HOLY
PRESENCE OF GOD ALMIGHTY?

I AM WAITING-
DO YOU NOT BELIEVE THAT YOU ARE IN THE HOLY
PRESENCE OF **CHRIST, THE KING?**

WHAT WILL YOUR **DECISION BE?**
WILL YOU HONOR THE HOLY REQUEST THAT WAS
PRODUCED BY ME?

I WANT YOU TO **ACKNOWLEDGE, YOU SEE-**
THE HOLY BIBLICAL WRITINGS THAT **CAME FROM ME.**

AS I WALK THROUGH YOUR CHURCHES PEW

ALMIGHTY GOD SPEAKING TO THE CLERGY TODAY

DEAR CLERGY; YOU LEADERS OF YOUR CHURCHES,
NOT MINE. AS I WALK THROUGH YOUR CHURCHES
FULL, **BUT EMPTY PEW.**
I CANNOT SEE ANY OF **MY FORETOLD CHOSEN FEW.**

I LOOK AROUND-
BUT, NOT ANY OF MY CHOSEN ONES, **COULD BE FOUND.**

I DO **NOT SEE-**

ANY CONGREGATION MEMBER WHO REALLY
RESPECT GOD, THE ALMIGHTY.

I DO **NOT BEHOLD-**
THE PRESENCE OF THE ONLY GOD WHO IS MORE
VALUABLE THAN **STORE BOUGHT CHEAP GOLD.**

AS I **WALK THROUGH-**
I CANNOT GRASP THE ABSENCE **OF MY CHOSEN FEW.**

WHERE ARE THEY? WHERE ARE THEY?
WHY DO YOU NOT INCLUDE IN YOUR CONGREGATIONS
THOSE WHO ACKNOWLEDGE AND FOLLOW **MY HOLY
LIFE-SAVING WAY?**

WHY, O MISGUIDED CLERGY?
WHY DO YOU NOT ACKNOWLEDGE THE HOLY
PRESENCE AND **WORDS OF ALMIGHTY ME?**

WHY DO **YOU MISLEAD-**
THOSE WHO CATER TO YOUR EARTHLY AND **HELL
BOUND GREED?**

WHY? WHY? WHY, O MISINFORMED CLERGY OF **THIS
PASSING WORLD?**
WHY DO YOU MISINFORM THE SPIRITUALLY
VULNERABLE LITTLE BOY AND GIRL?

DO YOU **NOT CARE?**
ARE YOU **FULLY AWARE?**

ARE YOU AWARE OF **THE PRICE?**
FOR YOU WILL BE TREATED LOWER THAT **YOUR CHURCHES UNFED MICE.**

PAY **CLOSE ATTENTION-**
FOR ALMIGHTY GOD WILL NOT LET YOUR FORM OF PREACHING DESTROY **HIS GREAT CREATION.**

PAY VERY **CLOSE ATTENTION-**
FOR, I WILL NEVER LET YOU LEAD MY VALUABLE ONES TO **SATAN'S REALM OF PERMANENT DESTRUCTION.**

PAY VERY CLOSE ATTENTION, **O MISLEADING CLERGY-**
FOR, I, ALMIGHTY GOD, WILL NOT ALLOW YOUR REAL OF LEADERSHIP TAKE FULL CONTROL OVER THE VULNERABLE ONES **WHO BELONGS TO ME.**

LISTEN! LISTEN! LISTEN TO ME-
LISTEN TO THE HOLY VOICE OF THE INFINITE **CHRIST JESUS, THE ALMIGHTY!**

FOR YOU HAVE BEEN **FOREWARNED BY ME-**

SO PAY VERY CLOSE ATTENTION TO **THE VOICE OF GOD, THE ALMIGHTY.**

YOU PUT ON A **FAKE GLORIOUS SHOW**-
FOR THOSE WHO DO **NOT REALLY KNOW.**

YOU PUT ON A FANTASTIC SHOW FOR THOSE WHO VISIT YOUR CHURCH TO GET **A GLIMPSE OF YOUR STAGE PERFORMANCE.**
BUT, YOU ALL DO NOT REALIZE THAT **I AM IN YOUR HELL BOUND DECEIVING PRESENCE.**

WHEN WILL **YOU WAKE UP**-
SO THAT YOU AND YOUR MISLED CONGREGATION MAY **DRINK FROM MY HEAVENLY CUP?**

WAKE UP! WAKE UP! **WAKE UP, O DECEITFUL CLERGY!**
WAKE UP, BEFORE YOU ENTER THE LAND OF THE DEAD **WITH SATAN, MY ENEMY!**

WAKE UP, DEAR CLERGY!
BEFORE YOU DANCE IN THE PIT WITH **MY DESTRUCTIVE ENEMY.**

TIME IS TICKING!
WAKE UP, O DECEIVING CLERGY, BEFORE YOU GET **A GREAT LICKING!!!**

TIME IS MOVING **VERY FAST**-
WAKE UP, O CLERGY, BEFORE YOUR MEMORY
BECOMES **A THING OF THE PAST!!!**

WAKE, O SPIRITUALLY **BLINDED CLERGY!**
WAKE UP, BEFORE YOU ARE JUDGED BY THE
FOREVER **LIVING CHRIST JESUS, THE ALMIGHTY!!!**

FOR, **YOUR JUDGEMENT DAY**-
IS APPROACHING YOUR **DECEIVING UNHOLY WAY!!!**

O CLERGY:
MOVE, MOVE, MOVE, VERY SWIFTLY!!!

YOUR LIMITED **TIME IS APPROACHING**-
FOR, NOW, YOU ARE IN THE HOLY PRESENCE OF
CHRIST **JESUS, YOUR FINAL JUDGE, GOD, AND KING!!!**

REPENT IN MY HOLY **PRESENCE, O CLERGY**-
FOR, I AM YOUR **FINAL JUDGE ALMIGHTY!!!**

REPENT! REPENT! REPENT, O CLERGY!
FOR, BELIEVE IT, OR NOT, YOU ARE IN THE HOLY
PRESENCE OF THE FINAL JUDGE; **CHRIST JESUS,
THE ALMIGHTY!!!**

FOR, **HOLY AND TRUE**-
IS THE ONE WHO WILL **JUDGE ALL OF YOU!!!**

Barbara Ann Mary Mack

THERE ARE NO EXCEPTIONS-
FOR, I WILL JUDGE ALL OF **EARTH'S DECEIVING NATIONS.**

FOR, HOLY, **ETERNAL AND REAL-**
IS THE PUNISHMENT THAT YOU WILL **ENCOUNTER AND FEEL!!!**

FOR, HOLY, **REAL, AND TRUE-**
IS THE GOD AND KING WHO **WILL SENTENCE YOU!!!**

HOLY, HOLY, HOLY-
IS THE GREAT AND FINAL JUDGE ALMIGHTY!!!

I MOVE, I MOVE, **I MOVE, YOU SEE-**
IN THE MIDST OF THE CHURCHES THAT BELONG TO THE WORLD'S **MISGUIDED AND MISLEADING CLERGY.**

HOLY AND TRUE-
IS THE SPIRIT THAT WATCHES OVER THE MANY MISLEADING THINGS **THAT YOU DO.**

I AM **OBSERVING-**
THE UNHOLY THINGS THAT YOU SAY AND DO IN THE PRESENCE OF CHRIST JESUS, **THE ETERNAL GOD AND KING.**

IT IS A GODLY **CRIME AND DISGRACE-**

THE WAY YOU DEFAME MY HOLINESS IN THE PRESENCE OF **MY INVISIBLE FACE.**

O CLERGY: I WILL NOT PERMIT **YOU TO DEFAME-** MY HOLY, ETERNAL, **LOVING NAME**

I WILL NOT ALLOW YOU DECEIVING ONES **TO SLANDER-** THE BELOVED NAME AND PRESENCE OF **ALMIGHTY GOD, YOUR CREATOR.**

FOR, YOU WILL **DEFINITELY PAY-** ON **JUDGEMENT DAY.**

THIS SAYS, **THE LORD GOD!!!** THIS SAYS, THE ORIGIN OF DIVINE **ETERNAL, MERCY AND LOVE!!!**

AND I WILL COMFORT AND PROTECT MY FAITHFUL AND DEVOTED CLERGY AND THEIR EARTHLY CHURCHES, SAYS THE LORD JESUS

<u>THE LORD JESUS SPEAKING TO HIS FAITHFUL AND DEVOTED EARTHLY CLERGY TODAY</u>

FOR, I WILL REAP- THE HOLY SOULS THAT I WILL KEEP.

O FAITHFUL **CLERGY OF MINE-**

I AM WITH YOU DURING THIS **TRYING PERIOD OF TIME.**

I WILL HEAL-
THE MANY SOULS THAT SATAN, OUR ENEMY, TRIES TO **DECEIVE AND STEAL.**

FOR, **HOLY AND TRUE-**
IS THE GOD AND SAVIOR WHO WALKS HAND IN HAND WITH **OBEDIENT AND FAITHFUL YOU.**

HOLY IS THE HEAVENLY THRONE THAT WAITS FOR BLESSED AND **BELOVED YOU.**
HOLY IS THE GOD WHO IS **ETERNAL AND TRUE.**

O **BELIEVING CLERGY-**
CONTINUE TO REPRESENT HOLY **LIFE REWARDING ME.**

FOR, I TOO-
AM **FAITHFUL TO YOU.**

BELIEVE! BELIEVE! BELIEVE!
FOR HEAVEN'S MANY REWARDS, YOU WILL **CERTAINLY RECEIVE!!!**

CONTINUE HONORING **MY GLORY-**
AS YOU REVEAL TO YOUR EARTHLY CONGREGATION, **MY HOLY ETERNAL LIFE SAVING STORY.**

LOOK UP TO ME-

LOOK UP TO YOUR GREAT ETERNAL REWARD (CHRIST JESUS), **O BLESSED CLERGY!!!**

FOR, **HOLY AND TRUE-**
IS THE GOD WHO HAS CALLED AND CHOSEN **BELOVED OBEDIENT YOU.**

MOVE WITH ME, O BELOVED FAITHFUL CLERGY WHO **LEADS MY LIFE SEEKING CHURCHES TODAY.**
MOVE WITH ALMIGHTY GOD, THE HOLY ONE, AS I GUIDE YOU AND YOUR CONGREGATIONS TO **MY EVERLASTING GLORIOUS WAY.**

FOLLOW, FOLLOW, **FOLLOW HOLY ME-**
FOLLOW ME, O BLESSED AND BELOVED **LIFE SEEKING CLERGY.**

FOR, **HOLY AND TRUE-**
IS THE GREAT KING WHO **LEADS OBEDIENT YOU!!!**

MY GLORIOUS WHITE ROBES **AWAITS, YOU SEE-**
FOR THE FAITHFUL CLERGY WHO **FOLLOWS ME.**
COME! COME! COME!
ENTER MY HOLY REALM, AS YOU BEHOLD **MY HEAVENLY HOME AND KINGDOM.**

FOR, HOLY, **REAL, AND TRUE-**

IS THE MIGHTY KING WHO **LEADS BLESSED YOU!!!**

FOLLOW ME, **O BLESSED ONES-**
AS YOU GUIDE MY LIFE SEEKING **DAUGHTERS AND SONS.**

FOR, **I, THE LORD JESUS-**
AM WATCHING OVER MY FAITHFUL AND OBEDIENT CLERGY, AS YOU GUIDE THE MEEK ONES **AND THE RIGHTEOUS.**

FOR, **HOLY AND TRUE-**
IS THE GOD WHO LOVES THE THINGS THAT YOU **PREACH AND DO!!!**

DEAR **CLERGY OF MINE-**
SEEK MY ETERNAL THRONE OF DIVINE PEACE AND GLORY DURING **THIS TRYING PERIOD OF TIME.**

SEEK ME-
AS YOU LEAD YOUR CONGREGATION TO **THE THRONE OF GOD ALMIGHTY.**

FOR, I, THE LORD **JESUS, DO DESIRE-**
TO LEAD YOUR CONGREGATION AWAY FROM HELL'S EVERLASTING **DESTRUCTION AND FIRE.**

I DESIRE TO SEE-

EVERY FACE THAT BELONGS TO THE GOD AND
HEAVENLY KING ALMIGHTY.

HOLY, HOLY, HOLY-
IS CHRIST JESUS, THE HEAVENLY GOD AND SAVIOR
ALMIGHTY!!!

FOR, HOLY AND TRUE-
IS THE KINGDOM AND GOD THAT WELCOME FAITHFUL
AND OBEDIENT YOU.

COME, O BLESSED CLERGY!
SIT BY THE SIDE OF CHRIST JESUS, THE ALMIGHTY.

JOIN ME TODAY-
AS YOU LEAD YOUR CONGREGATIONS TO MY BLESSED
EVERLASTING HOLY WAY!!!

FOR, HOLY AND TRUE-
IS THE GOD WHO SEES HIS FAITHFUL CLERGY
THROUGH.

ALLELUIA!!!

BOOK THREE

KNOCKING ON HEAVEN'S DOOR

SUBTITLE
MAY I ENTER, DEAR GOD?

BY:

BARBARA ANN MARY MACK

BEHOLD MY PRESENT TESTAMENT, THE CONTINUANCE OF MY OLD AND NEW TESTAMENTS, *SAYS THE LORD GOD*

BY:

BARBARA ANN MARY MACK

BEGAN AUGUST 5, 2024
COMPLETED: AUGUST 9, 2024

DEDICATION

TO CHRIST *JESUS,* A TRUE SERVANT OF GOD, THE
FATHER

ACKNOWLEDGMENT

ACKNOWLEDGING CHRIST *JESUS'* TRUE IDENTITY AS GOD, THE SON

PROLOGUE

I WILL ENTER HEAVEN'S SWEET DOOR THAT LEADS TO THE MIGHTY THRONE OF THE BLESSED WELL-LOVED HOLY TRINITY. I WILL ENTER WITH DIVINE GLADNESS, AS I APPROACH THE THRONE THAT WAITS FOR BLESSED ME. I WILL MOVE IN THE MIDST OF GOD'S HOLINESS AND GRACE, AS I LOOK UPON HIS HOLY ETERNAL PRESENCE AND FACE. WITH GREAT REVERENCE, I WILL SIT UPON THE THRONE THAT IS PLACED BETWEEN GOD, THE FATHER'S, AND GOD, THE SON'S, HOLY THRONES. I WILL SIT UPON MY THRONE, AS I GIVE REVERENCE TO GOD, THE FATHER, AND CHRIST JESUS, HIS ONLY BEGOTTEN SON. MY KNOCK WAS WELCOMED BY THE BLESSED TRINITY, AS THE THREE IN ONE, GREETED ME WITH DIVINE LOVE AND GRATITUDE. FOR, GOD, THE FATHER, AND CHRIST JESUS, HIS ONLY BEGOTTEN SON, AND GOD, THE HOLY SPIRIT, AGREE IN EVERYTHING, WHICH MAKES THEM ONE ESSENCE AND ONE ENTITY; ONE GOD. HOLY, HOLY, HOLY, IS ALMIGHTY GOD, THE BELOVED TRINITY. FOR HE ACCEPTS THOSE WHO HUMBLY PRESENT HIMSELF, OR HERSELF TO HIM. HOLY, HOLY, HOLY, IS

THE UNITY OF GOD ALMIGHTY!!! I HAVE ENTERED HEAVEN'S OPEN DOOR IN THE PRESENCE OF GOD'S HOLY ANGELS AND PURIFIED SAINTS. I HAVE BEEN PRIVILEGED TO BEHOLD HEAVEN'S VASTNESS AND PURITY. OH, WHAT AN HONORABLE AND AWESOME EXPERIENCE; AND PERMANENT PLACE TO BEHOLD THROUGHOUT SWEET ETERNITY. HOLY, HOLY, HOLY, IS THE ETERNAL DWELLING PLACE OF GOD ALMIGHTY!!!

INTRODUCTION

BEHOLD ALMIGHTY GOD'S HEAVENLY RESIDENCE, DEAR BARBARA

ALMIGHTY GOD, THE FATHER, SPEAKING TO BARBARA AS SHE ENTER'S HEAVEN'S OPEN DOOR

ENTER MY OPEN DOOR, **DEAR BARBARA**-
ENTER THE HOME THAT HAS BEEN CALLED INTO EXISTENCE BY ALMIGHTY GOD, YOUR BELOVED **ORIGIN, CREATOR, AND DIVINE FATHER.**

ENTER WITH GLADNESS, **DEAR ONE**-
AS YOU GREET GOD, THE FATHER'S, **ONLY BEGOTTEN WORTHY SON.**

ENTER WITH **DIVINE JOY**-
AS YOU ENTER THE HOME THAT THE REALM OF DESTRUCTION COULD **NEVER ENTER NOR DESTROY.**

ENTER MY HOLY GATE, **DEAR DAUGHTER.**
ENTER THE HOME THAT WAS CREATED BY **GOD, YOUR FATHER.**

ENTER, ENTER, ENTER-

ENTER MY BLESSED HOME ON HIGH, O BLESSED AND **WORTHY DAUGHTER.**

FOR, **HOLY, YOU SEE**-
IS THE HOME AND DWELLING PLACE OF THE **ETERNAL GOD ALMIGHTY.**

I HEARD YOUR SWEET KNOCK, **DEAR DAUGHTER**-
I HEARD THE KNOCK THAT CAME FROM THE BLESSED BEING OF **MY HEAVEN INVITED MESSENGER.**

ENTER THE **GATES**-
FOR, YOUR HEAVENLY **THRONE AWAITS.**

ENTER THE HEAVENLY JOY THAT **SURROUNDS YOU**-
AS YOU GREET THE HOLY ONE WHO IS **ETERNAL, FAITHFUL AND TRUE.**

ENTER, ENTER, ENTER-
ENTER HEAVEN'S OPEN DOOR, **DEAR OBEDIENT DAUGHTER.**

DEAR BARBARA: **COME INSIDE**-
FOR, IN SWEET HEAVEN, THE RESIDENTS AND I EXPRESS AND LOVE AND PEACE, WHICH **WE REFUSE TO DENY AND HIDE.**

COME, **DEAR BARBARA.**

COME AND SIT WITH US, DEAR **WORTHY DAUGHTER.**

FOR, I LONG TO **BEHOLD AND SEE-**
THE BELOVED DAUGHTER WHO WAS CALLED AND
CHOSEN **BY HOLY ETERNAL ME.**

COME, **DEAR BARBARA.**
COME, AND SIT ON THE THRONE THAT IS PLACED **BY
GOD, YOUR HEAVENLY GUIDE AND FATHER.**

COME, DEAR ONE-
AND SIT ON YOUR THRONE THAT IS VERY NEAR TO
ALMIGHTY GOD, THE FATHER, AND THE LORD **JESUS,
MY ONLY BEGOTTEN SON.**

COME, DEAR **HEAVEN SENT QUEEN-**
THERE, YOU WILL BEHOLD AN EXPERIENCE THAT
NO OTHER HUMAN BEING HAS SEEN.

COME-
AND ENJOY THE SURROUNDINGS OF **MY VAST
HEAVENLY KINGDOM.**

COME, DEAR **LOVELY BARBARA-**
AND ANSWER THE CALL OF GOD, YOUR LONGED FOR
ORIGIN AND FATHER.

TAKE MY HOLY **OUTSTRETCHED HAND-**

SO THAT MY HOLY SPIRIT AND PRESENCE MAY LEAD
YOU TO **MY PROMISED DWELLING PLACE AND LAND.**

BARBARA SPEAKING TO GOD, THE FATHER

MY GOD: MY FIRST AND **ETERNAL LOVE-**
O HOLY ONE WHO DESCENDED TO US FROM **SWEET
HEAVEN ABOVE.**

O HOLY **DELIGHT-**
O GREAT AND EVERLASTING **CONTINUOUS LIGHT.**

O BLESSED ONE-
O VICTOR IN EVERY BATTLE THAT **HAS BEGUN.**

O GREAT **MIGHT-**
O FATHER WHO KEEPS HIS LOVED ONES WITHIN **HIS
DIVINE SIGHT.**

O HOLY **CREATOR-**
O PERFECT **GOD AND SAVIOR.**

I TRULY-
ADORE EVERYTHING THAT IS **GOOD AND HOLY.**

O DIVINE **STRENGTH OF MINE-**
O BLESSED ORIGIN OF **UNENDING TIME.**

O REALM OF **HOLINESS-**

O BLESSED SAVIOR WHO RELEASES DAILY, **DIVINE GOODNESS.**

MY BLESSED SOUL **STANDS BEFORE-**
HEAVEN'S OPEN **WELCOMING DOOR.**

WITH MY BLESSED SPIRIT **LOW TO THE GROUND-**
I SEEK THE SAVIOR WHO IS **ALWAYS AROUND.**

HOLY ARE YOU, O SWEET **DELIGHTFUL ETERNITY-**
O BLESSED ONE WHO HAS SAVED YOUR HEAVEN BOUND **LOVED ONES AND ME.**

REACH FOR ME-
REACHED FOR THE BLESSED DAUGHTER AND MESSENGER OF THE **INFINITE GOD ALMIGHTY.**

HERE I AM; KNOCKING ON SWEET **HEAVEN'S HOLY DOOR.**
FOR, I WILL ENTER EARTH'S GATES **NO MORE.**

I HAVE **EXITED, YOU SEE-**
THE EARTHLY GATES THAT BROUGHT TERROR TO **YOU AND ME.**

HOLY, HOLY, HOLY-
ARE THE HEAVENLY GATES THAT LEAD TO THE THRONE OF GOD ALMIGHTY!!!

CHAPTER ONE

I CAN REALLY SEE IT!

BARBARA SPEAKING

I CAN SEE IT! I CAN SEE IT! I CAN REALLY AND
TRULY SEE IT!
I CAN SEE IT, BY THE POWER OF **ALMIGHTY GOD'S
HOLY SPIRIT!**

FOR, IT ISN'T **TOO FAR-**
I CAN SEE IT! FOR IT ISN'T WAY ABOVE **THE FARTHEST
STAR.**

I CAN SEE IT, FOR IT ISN'T **TOO FAR AWAY-**
I CAN SEE IT ON THE BRIGHTEST OR **GLOOMY DAY.**

I CAN SEE IT, FOR, IT IS MY **HOME AND DESTINATION.**
I CAN REALLY SEE IT, FOR IT IS **GOD'S WONDERFUL
CREATION.**

I CAN SEE IT, FOR IT IS **BEYOND THE MOON.**
I CAN REALLY SEE THE PLACE THAT I WILL **RESIDE
VERY SOON.**

I CAN SEE IT!

FOR, IT IS SURROUNDED WITH GOD'S **HOLY PRESENCE AND SPIRIT.**

I CAN SEE THE PLACE OF **MY DESTINATION-**
I CAN SEE THE GLORIOUS PLACE WHERE GOD HAS PREPARED **A PLACE FOR EVERY NATION.**

FOR, **HOLY AND TRUE-**
IS THE PLACE THAT GOD HAS **PREPARED FOR ME AND YOU.**

HEAVEN, HEAVEN; SWEET UNENDING **REALM CALLED HEAVEN.**
SWEET HEAVEN IS MY LONGED FOR **EVERLASTING DESTINATION.**

SWEET HEAVEN-
IS THE DESTINATION OF GOD'S CHOSEN AND **BLESSED CREATION.**

I WILL **LOOK FOR IT-**
WITH THE HELP AND GUIDANCE OF **GOD'S HOLY SPIRIT.**

I WILL LOOK FOR THE PLACE WHERE I CAN REST MY **WEARY HEAD AND SPIRIT.**
AND, I WILL SING VERY LOUD, SO THAT THE OPEN GATES OF SWEET **HEAVEN CAN HEAR IT.**

I WILL **SING, SING, SING**-
AS I LISTEN FOR THE HOLY VOICE OF CHRIST JESUS,
THE FOREVER REIGNING KING.

I WILL LISTEN FOR **THE SOUND**-
THAT LETS ME KNOW THAT THE REALM OF **HOLINESS
IS AROUND.**

I WILL LISTEN FOR THE HOLY **VOICE OF GOD
ALMIGHTY**-
I WILL LISTEN FOR THE HOLY SPIRIT THAT
BECKONS ME.

I WILL **LISTEN, YOU SEE**-
FOR THE HOLY VOICE OF THE HEAVENLY GOD WHO
CREATED BLESSED ME.

I WILL LISTEN; I **WILL LISTEN**-
I WILL LISTEN FOR THE SOUND OF SWEET VICTORY
AND **DIVINE SALVATION.**

I WILL KNOCK ON HEAVEN'S OPEN DOOR BEFORE MY
BLESSED **SOUL AND SPIRIT ENTER.**
I WILL LOOK FOR THE HOLY PRESENCE OF ALMIGHTY
GOD, **MY HEAVENLY CREATOR AND FATHER.**

I WILL **LOOK AROUND**-
AS I LISTEN FOR THE HOLY **UNINTERRUPTED SOUND.**

And I Was Told That He, Christ Jesus, Is God Also   73

FOR, I WANT TO **WITNESS AND SEE-**
GOD'S DIVINE **HEAVENLY BEAUTY.**

HOLY, HOLY, HOLY-
IS THE UNENDING PRESENCE OF GOD ALMIGHTY!!!

MY DESTINATION

MY DESTINATION: MY SWEET **LONGED FOR DESTINATION-**
IS TO THE HEAVENLY HOME OF **MY PROMISED SALVATION.**

I WILL BE VERY **GOOD, YOU SEE-**
SO THAT I MAY SEE AND COMPLETE **MY LONGED FOR DESTINY.**

FOR, **HOLY, YOU SEE-**
IS THE HEAVENLY REALM THAT **WAITS FOR ME.**

I WILL BOW, AS I KNOCK ON **HEAVEN'S OPEN DOOR.**
FOR, MY BLESSED SPIRIT NEEDS **TO SEARCH NO MORE.**

HOLY, HOLY, HOLY-
IS MY DESTINATION TO THE HEAVENLY HOME OF GOD ALMIGHTY!!!

FOR, **HOLY, YOU SEE**-
IS MY **HEAVEN BOUND DESTINY.**

I CAN SEE! I CAN SEE! **I CAN SEE**-
THE HOLY ANGELS OF **GOD ALMIGHTY!**

MY GRATEFUL SOUL **DOES REJOICE**-
AS I LISTEN FOR MY SAVIOR'S **HOLY INVITING VOICE.**

FOR, **HOLY, YOU SEE**-
IS THE VOICE THAT HAS CALLED OUT TO **BLESSED
OBEDIENT ME.**

THE SACRED DOOR TO MY HUMBLED HEART **HAS
OPENED WIDE**-
FOR, I HAVE KNOCKED ON THE DOOR THAT HAS
RELEASED A LOVE THAT **I REFUSE TO ABANDON
OR HIDE.**

FOR, ALMIGHTY GOD **JEHOVAH, YOU SEE**-
HAS CAPTURED THE MIND, BODY, AND HEART THAT
HE HAS GIVEN TO ME.

HOLY, HOLY, HOLY-
IS MY LOVING **GOD ALMIGHTY!!!**

I HAVE KNOCKED ON HEAVEN'S OPEN DOOR TODAY

BARBARA SPEAKING

I HAVE KNOCKED ON HEAVEN'S **OPEN DOOR TODAY-**
I WILL ENTER MY NEW PLACE OF RESIDENCE AS **MY SOUL AND SPIRIT PRAY.**

I WILL SING TUNES THAT **ARE MELODIOUS-**
AS I LISTEN FOR THE HOLY VOICE OF **LIFE SAVING KING JESUS.**

FOR, **HOLY, YOU SEE-**
IS THE CHRIST AND GOD WHO **WELCOMED BLESSED ME.**

HOLY, HOLY, HOLY-
IS THE LIVING SPIRIT OF CHRIST JESUS, THE ALMIGHTY!!!

I CAN HEAR YOUR KNOCK, DEAR BARBARA, SAYS THE LORD GOD

THE LORD GOD SPEAKING TO BARBARA, HIS SENT MESSENGER AND DAUGHTER

I CAN HEAR YOUR SILENT **KNOCK, DEAR BARBARA.**
COME! AND ENTER THE HEAVEN PREPARED HOME OF **GOD, YOUR MIGHTY LOVING FATHER.**

I CAN HEAR YOUR **SILENT KNOCK OF LOVE-**
AS YOU JOIN ME IN **THE HEAVENS ABOVE.**

I CAN **HEAR YOU-**
I CAN FEEL THE LOVE THAT IS **EVERLASTING AND TRUE.**

FOR, **HOLY, YOU SEE-**
IS THE LOVE THAT YOU **SHARE WITH GOD ALMIGHTY.**

AND, I HEARD YOUR LOVELY KNOCK, DEAR BARBARA, SAYS THE LORD GOD

ALMIGHTY GOD SPEAKING TO BARBARA

I, THE LORD **GOD, YOU SEE-**
HAVE HEARD THE SILENT KNOCK ON HEAVEN'S SWEET DOOR THAT CAME FROM THE SANCTIFIED HANDS OF THE DAUGHTER WHO WAS **BLESSED BY ME.**

I HEARD, **YOU SEE-**
THE BEAUTY THAT **DESCENDED FROM ME.**

FOR, YOU, **DEAR BARBARA-**
ARE MY WELL-LOVED **QUEEN AND DAUGHTER.**

I HEARD YOUR LOVELY SILENT **KNOCK, DEAR BARBARA.**

I HEARD THE GLORIOUS SOUND THAT CAME FROM THE GOD FORMED **HANDS OF MY OBEDIENT MESSENGER.**

YOUR KNOCK WAS **VERY LOUD AND CLEAR**-
IT WAS A SILENT KNOCK THAT ONLY HEAVEN'S RESIDENTS AND **INVITED GUESTS COULD HEAR.**

YOUR KNOCK WAS **LOUD AND CLEAR**-
YES, DEAR BARBARA! YOUR LOVELY KNOCK ON HEAVEN'S DOOR **COULD BE HEARD EVERYWHERE.**

YOUR SILENT KNOCK WAS **LOUD AND CLEAR**-
IT WAS A GLORIOUS KNOCK THAT **WAS VERY NEAR.**

HOLY, HOLY, HOLY-
ARE THE KNOCKING HANDS THAT WERE CALLED INTO EXISTENCE BY GOD ALMIGHTY!!!

FOR, BARBARA'S SANCTIFIED **HANDS, YOU SEE**-
FUSED WITH BLESSED **LIFE GIVING ME.**

HOLY, HOLY, HOLY-
ARE THE POWER AND UNIFICATION OF BARBARA AND GOD ALMIGHTY!!!

FOR, **HOLY AND TRUE**-

IS THE KNOCK THAT CAME FROM **BLESSED YOU.**

AND HEAVEN'S SWEET DOORS OPENED WIDE FOR THE EXIT AND DELIVERY OF GOD'S HOLY WORDS TODAY

<u>**BARBARA SPEAKING TO HEAVEN'S OPEN DOORS**</u>

AND, HEAVEN'S SWEET DOORS OPENED WIDE FOR THE **EXIT AND DELIVERY OF GOD'S HOLY WORDS TODAY.**
FOR, EARTH'S BELIEVING RESIDENTS ARE EAGER TO HEAR WHAT **THE ALMIGHTY HAS TO SAY.**

OH HOLY DOOR-
YOU HAVE OPENED WIDE, SO THAT YOU MAY RECEIVE AND WELCOME THE BLESSED SOULS OF **THE RICH AND THE POOR.**

YOU HEARD MY HUMBLED SILENT KNOCK AT **YOUR HOLY DOOR-**
AND NOW, MY BLESSED SPIRIT NEEDS TO WAIT FOR **MY ENTRANCE ANY MORE.**

HOLY, HOLY, HOLY-
ARE THE SILENT KNOCKS THAT CAME FROM THE HANDS OF BARBARA; THE SENT MESSENGER OF GOD ALMIGHTY!!!

O BLESSED DOORS; YOU HAVE OPENED WIDE FOR
ME, **THE FAITHFUL ONE.**
AND NOW, I WANT TO ENTER THE HEAVENLY JOY
THAT **HAS ALREADY BEGUN.**

HOLY, HOLY, HOLY-
ARE THE JOYFUL SOUNDS THAT PERMEATE THE
HEAVENLY HOME OF GOD ALMIGHTY!!!

COME IN, DEAR BARBARA!

<u>**ALMIGHTY GOD SPEAKING TO BARBARA, HIS SENT
MESSENGER AND DAUGHTER**</u>

COME IN, DEAR BARBARA!
ENTER THE HEAVENLY HOME THAT WAS CALLED
INTO EXISTENCE BY ALMIGHTY GOD, YOUR BLESSED
AND **BELOVED ORIGIN AND FATHER.**

COME IN, DEAR BARBARA!
NOW, YOUR BLESSED SOUL AND SPIRIT, MAY BE
SEATED NEXT TO **ME, DEAR DAUGHTER.**

FOR, YOUR HEAVENLY **THRONE AWAITS-**
FOR THE MESSENGER AND DAUGHTER WHO JUST
ENTERED **HEAVEN'S OPENED GATES.**

SIT NEXT TO ME-

YES, DEAR BARBARA! YOU MAY BE SEATED NEXT TO **GOD, THE ALMIGHTY.**

SIT NEXT TO ME-
I WANT YOU TO SIT NEXT TO THE ESSENCE OF DIVINE LOVE WHO **HAS SET YOU FREE.**

SIT NEXT TO **THE HOLY FATHER AND GOD-**
WHO PROMISED YOU A WONDERFUL TASTE OF HIS REALM OF **UNENDING DIVINE LOVE.**

LOOK UNTO ME-
FOR, I HAVE TRULY SET YOUR BELOVED AND **BLESSED SPIRIT FREE!!!**

HOLY, HOLY, HOLY-
ARE THE UNITED AND FUSED SPIRITS OF BARBARA AND GOD, THE ALMIGHTY!!!

DEAR BARBARA: SIT HERE BY **MY HOLY SIDE-**
SO THAT WE MAY EXPRESS A DIVINE UNION THAT **YOU AND I CANNOT HIDE.**

FOR, **HOLY AND TRUE-**
IS THE LOVE THAT I HAVE FOR OBEDIENT **AND FAITHFUL YOU.**

HOLY, HOLY, HOLY-

IS THE LOVE OF CHRIST ALMIGHTY!!!

FOR, IT IS PERFECT, AND **IT IS STRONG.**
IT IS A DIVINE LOVE THAT CARRIES US **ALL THE DAY LONG.**

DEAR DAUGHTER: SIT NEXT TO ME ON YOUR GOD MADE **THRONE OF DIVINE LOVE.** FOR, IT HAS WAITED FOR YOU TO ASCEND TO **SWEET HEAVEN ABOVE.**

DEAR BARBARA: YOU HAVE ENTERED **MY HEAVENLY HOME ABOVE.**
AND NOW, YOU AND I MAY EXHIBIT OUR REALM OF **UNENDING HEAVENLY BLISSFUL LOVE.**

FOR, **HOLY AND TRUE–**
IS MY **LOVE FOR YOU.**

BARBARA SPEAKING

MY BODY AND SOUL **KNOCK, YOU SEE**
ON THE DIVINE HEAVENLY DOOR THAT LEADS TO **THE THRONE OF GOD ALMIGHTY.**

I KNOCK, **AND I KNOCK.**
MY SOUL AND BODY KNOCK ON THE DOOR THAT DOESN'T HAVE **A PHYSICAL LOCK.**

I WILL **WAIT, YOU SEE-**
FOR THE WELCOMING VOICE OF THE FOREVER-LIVING
CHRIST JESUS, THE ALMIGHTY.

I WILL **NOT ENTER-**
UNTIL I SEE THE WELCOMING FACE OF CHRIST
ALMIGHTY, **MY LOVE AND SAVIOR.**

MY BLESSED SOUL **KNOCKS, YOU SEE-**
FOR, I WANT **TO BE FREE.**

FREE! FREE! FREE-
I WANT TO BE SEPARATED FROM THE WORLD THAT
BLINDS HEAVEN SENT ME.

FREE! FREE! FREE-
I WANT TO LIVE IN SWEET HEAVEN ABOVE WITH
THE BLESSED TRINITY.

**HEAVEN'S HOLY DOOR WAITS FOR MY HUMBLE
KNOCK**

BARBARA SPEAKING TO THE LORD JESUS

CAN YOU HEAR MY SOUL AS IT KNOCKS ON **HEAVEN'S
HOLY DOOR?**
CAN YOU HEAR THE CONTINUOUS **KNOCK OF THE
POOR?**

ALTHOUGH I AM RICH IN **YOUR DIVINE LOVE-**
MY POOR SPIRIT AND SOUL LONG FOR MY THRONE,
WHICH SITS NEXT TO YOURS IN **SWEET HEAVEN ABOVE.**

LISTEN, LISTEN, LISTEN FOR MY HOLY KNOCK, **LORD JESUS.**
LISTEN FOR THE KNOCK OF **YOUR RIGHTEOUS.**

FOR, **I AM WEARY-**
AND, MY BATTERED SOUL LONGS FOR THE HOLY
REALM OF SWEET **INFINITY; GOD ALMIGHTY.**

WILL YOU HEAR AND HONOR MY HUMBLE **KNOCK, LORD JESUS?**
WILL YOU OPEN HEAVEN'S DOOR TO **THOSE WHO ARE PRECIOUS?**

WILL YOU LET MY **BLESSED SOUL ENTER-**
SO THAT I MAY HAVE AN EVERLASTING LIFE WITH
GOD, **MY FOREVER-LIVING SAVIOR?**

LORD JESUS: **MAY I ENTER?**
MAY I SIT ON THE THRONE NEXT TO ALMIGHTY GOD,
MY LIVING KING AND SAVIOR?

LORD GOD-

MAY I ENTER SWEET HEAVEN, SO THAT MY BLESSED
SPIRIT MAY **SIT BY YOUR HOLY SIDE?**

FATHER GOD: **MAY I? MAY I?**
MAY I DWELL WITH YOU IN THE HEAVENS ABOVE
THE FLOURISHING BLUE SKY?

FOR, **HOLY AND TRUE-**
IS THE THRONE THAT SITS NEXT TO **BELOVED YOU.**

**I CAN HEAR GOD'S HEAVENLY ANGELS AS I KNOCK
ON HEAVEN'S HOLY DOOR**

BARBARA SPEAKING

I CAN HEAR! I CAN HEAR!
I CAN HEAR GOD'S HOLY ANGELS, FOR **THEY ARE
VERY NEAR.**

I CAN HEAR THEIR **MELODIOUS SOUND-**
AS THEY SOFTLY **MOVE AROUND.**

THEY ARE VERY QUIET AND **SWIFT, YOU SEE-**
FOR, THEY ARE THE **ANGELS OF GOD ALMIGHTY.**

I CAN HEAR YOU, O BLESSED OF **THE MOST HIGH.**

I CAN HEAR YOUR MARVELOUS SOUNDS AS YOU MOVE WITHIN **THE DWELLING PLACE ABOVE THE BRIGHT BLUE SKY.**

CAN YOU HEAR **ME KNOCKING?**
CAN YOU HEAR ME AS GOD'S **HOLY CHOIRS SING?**

CAN YOU HEAR ME? **CAN YOU HEAR ME?**
CAN YOU HEAR ME KNOCKING ON **HEAVEN'S SWEET DOOR?**

CAN YOU HEAR ME KNOCKING ON THE HEAVENLY DOOR OF **THE BLESSED HOLY TRINITY?**
CAN YOU HEAR ME KNOCK ON THE HEAVENLY **DOOR OF GOD ALMIGHTY?**

HOLY, HOLY, HOLY-
IS THE DOOR THAT LEADS TO GOD ALMIGHTY.

MY BLESSED **SOUL IS KNOCKING-**
ON HEAVEN'S HOLY DOOR. FOR I WANT TO MEET AND GREET JESUS CHRIST, FOR **HE IS OUR SOVEREIGN GOD AND KING.**

I WANT YOU TO **RECEIVE ME-**
FOR, I AM A MESSENGER OF **GOD, THE FATHER, ALMIGHTY!!!**

DEAR HEAVENLY FATHER AND GOD OF MINE:
PLEASE HONOR **THE KNOCKS YOU SEE-**
OF THE FAITHFUL **DAUGHTER OF GOD ALMIGHTY.**

FOR, **HOLY, YOU SEE-**
IS THE HEAVENLY HOME OF **GOD, THE ALMIGHTY!**

**THE HOLY KNOCK THAT AWAKES ME THROUGHOUT
EACH BLESSED DAY**

BARBARA SPEAKING

THE HOLY KNOCK THAT **AWAKES ME EVERY DAY-**
IS THE KNOCK THAT LEADS ME TO CHRIST **JESUS'
HOLY LIFE-SAVING WAY.**

I CAN HEAR! **I CAN REALLY HEAR-**
THE SOUND OF MY GOD AND SAVIOR WHOSE HOLY
PRESENCE IS VERY NEAR.

FOR, HE **KNOCKS, YOU SEE-**
ON THE DOOR OF THE HEART THAT BELONGS TO
BLESSED OBEDIENT ME.

HOLY, HOLY, HOLY-
IS THE KNOCK OF JEHOVAH GOD ALMIGHTY!!!

I HAVE OPENED THE DOOR TO MY HEART OF SACRED
HEAVEN ORDERED LOVE

BARBARA SPEAKING

I HAVE OPENED THE DOOR TO MY HEART OF LOVE-
SO THAT I MAY SEE THE DIVINE ESSENCE OF THE
GOD WHO DESCENDED TO ME FROM SWEET HEAVEN
ABOVE.

ENTER! ENTER! ENTER, O HOLY LAND!
ENTER MY OPEN HEART, BY THE POWER AND LOVE
OF YOUR HOLY HAND.

FOR, HOLY AND REAL-
IS YOUR KNOCK THAT I CAN REALLY FEEL.

HOLY, HOLY, HOLY AND TRUE-
IS THE HEAVENLY KNOCK THAT COMES WITH YOU.

AND WHEN GOD'S HOLY KNOCK REACHES MY
HUMBLED DOOR

BARBARA SPEAKING

WHEN GOD'S HOLY KNOCK REACHES MY DOOR-
I WILL GIVE PRAISE TO THE HOLY ONE WHOM MY
BLESSED SPIRIT WAS LOOKING FOR.

Barbara Ann Mary Mack

FOR, **HOLY AND REAL**-
IS THE PRESENCE THAT MY HUMBLED HEART **CAN TRULY FEEL.**

BARBARA SPEAKING TO CHRIST JESUS, THE ALMIGHTY

KNOCK. KNOCK, KNOCK ON MY HEART OF LOVE, **DEAR BLESSED SAVIOR.**
FOR, YOU HAVE ENTERED THE HEART OF **YOUR OBEDIENT DAUGHTER.**

OH HOW I LOOK **FORWARD TO**-
BEING AND DINING **WITH HOLY YOU.**

OH, HOW **I DESIRE**-
TO BE WITH A LOVE THAT WILL **NEVER GROW OLD NOR TIRE.**

FOR, **HOLY AND TRUE**-
IS THE LOVE THAT I SHARE WITH GOD, THE FATHER, **AND ALMIGHTY YOU.**

OH, HOW **I LONG, YOU SEE**-
TO BE WITH GOD, THE FATHER, **THROUGHOUT SWEET ETERNITY.**

WHEN MY THOUGHTS ROAM THIS WHOLE WIDE
WORLD AND THE SWEET HEAVENS ABOVE

BARBARA SPEAKING

WHEN MY SPIRITUAL THOUGHTS ROAM THIS WORLD
AND **THE SWEET HEAVENS ABOVE.**
MY BLESSED SOUL CLINGS TO THE ONE WHOM I
TRULY LOVE.

WHEN MY HOLY THOUGHTS MOVE IN THE DIRECTION
OF **THE FOREVER-LIVING CHRIST JESUS-**
I GIVE A SPIRITUAL TOAST TO THE KING OF THE
FAITHFUL, OBEDIENT ONES, **AND THE RIGHTEOUS.**

FOR, **HOLY AND TRUE-**
IS THE GOD OVER **ME AND YOU.**

WHEN MY BLESSED SOUL LOOKS UP TOWARD
HEAVEN'S OPEN DOOR-
I REMINISCE OVER THE THINGS THAT I **SEARCH FOR
NO MORE.**

FOR, I TRULY **ADORE, YOU SEE-**
EVERYONE WHO CALLS OUT TO **GOD ALMIGHTY.**

FOR, **HOLY AND REAL-**

IS THE HEAVEN SENT GOD THAT I CAN **TRULY SEE AND FEEL.**

OH MY LOVE: OH LONGED FOR SWEET HEAVEN ABOVE

BARBARA SPEAKING TO ALMIGHTY GOD

OH, MY ETERNAL **GOD OF LOVE-**
OH LONGED FOR **SWEET HEAVEN ABOVE.**

YOU, O HOLY ONE-
SHINES THROUGH MY BLESSED BEING WITH THE RADIANCE THAT IS BESTOWED UPON GOD, THE **FATHER'S, ONLY BEGOTTEN SON.**

FOR, YOU, O **LONGED FOR LORD JESUS-**
ARE TRULY **VALUABLE, PRICELESS, AND PRECIOUS.**

AND WHEN HEAVEN'S SWEET BELLS SOUND

BARBARA SPEAKING

WHEN HEAVEN'S SWEET BELLS **RING, RING, RING!!!**
I KNOW THAT MY BLESSED BEING IS IN THE HOLY PRESENCE OF CHRIST **JESUS, THE ONE AND ONLY HOLY GOD AND REIGNING KING.**

AND WHEN HEAVEN'S **SWEET BELLS SOUND-**
I KNOW THAT GOD'S HOLY **SPIRIT IS AROUND.**

FOR, HE IS ALMIGHTY GOD, **THE HEAVENLY KING-**
AND HIS HOLY PRESENCE MAKES MY SPIRIT AND
SOUL **DANCE AND SING.**

FOR, **HOLY, YOU SEE-**
IS THE GOD AND KING WHO REIGNS IN THE PRESENCE
OF **EARTH'S RESIDENTS AND ME.**

HOLY, HOLY, HOLY-
IS GOD, THE HEAVENLY KING ALMIGHTY!!!

HE MOVES IN OUR BLESSED MIDST **WITH DIVINE
STYLE-**
HE WILL GRACE US WITH HIS HOLY **PRESENCE ON
EARTH FOR A WHILE.**

AS WE ENTER HEAVEN'S OPEN DOOR

BARBARA SPEAKING

AS WE ENTER **HEAVEN'S OPEN DOOR-**
WE HAVE NO NEED TO LOOK FOR **THE DIVINE ONE
ANY MORE.**

HOLY IS CHRIST JESUS, THE EVERLASTING **KING OF
KINGS-**
WHO SURROUNDS HIS INVITED GUESTS WITH **GOOD
HEAVENLY THINGS.**

HOLY IS **THE KING-**
HOLY ARE THE HEAVENLY **CHOIRS THAT SING.**

SING! SING! SING!
SING, O GREAT HEAVENLY MULTITUDE, AS YOU
GREET CHRIST JESUS, **OUR FOREVER REIGNING GOD
AND VICTORIOUS KING!**

SING! SING! SING! SING, **O HOLY RESIDENTS OF SWEET
HEAVEN!**
SING IN THE PRESENCE OF ALMIGHTY GOD, AND **HIS
GRATEFUL CHOSEN!**

HOLY, HOLY, HOLY-
IS THE BLESSED DOOR THAT LEADS TO THE
HEAVENLY HOME OF GOD ALMIGHTY!!!

OH HEAVEN SENT ONE

**BARBARA SPEAKING TO THE FOREVER-LIVING
CHRIST JESUS**

OH HEAVEN SENT ONE: YOU ALWAYS CHEER ME UP
WHEN **MY SPIRIT AND SOUL FEEL DOWN.**
FOR, YOUR HOLY SPIRIT AND PRESENCE **ARE
ALWAYS AROUND.**

YOUR HOLY SPIRIT **CONSTANTLY SPEAKS TO ME-**

AS YOU REVEAL **YOUR RADIANT BEAUTY.**

FOR, **HOLY AND REAL-**
IS YOUR PRESENCE THAT I CAN **TRULY SEE AND FEEL.**

HOLY, HOLY, HOLY-
IS THE FOREVER-LIVING LORD GOD ALMIGHTY!!!

IF HEAVEN COULD SEE ME NOW

<u>**BARBARA SPEAKING**</u>

IF THE OPEN GATES TO SWEET HEAVEN **COULD SEE ME-**
THEY WOULD RECEIVE THE **MESSENGER OF GOD ALMIGHTY.**

IF SWEET HEAVEN COULD SEE ME NOW, **ITS EXISTENCE-**
WOULD REVEAL **GOD'S HOLY PRESENCE.**

IF SWEET HEAVEN **COULD SEE ME-**
IT WOULD REJOICE WITH ALMIGHTY GOD, THE SACRED AND **BLESSED TRINITY.**

IF SWEET HEAVEN **COULD SEE ME NOW-**
GOD'S HOLY ANGELS WOULD **WELCOME ME ANYHOW.**

IF SWEET HEAVEN **COULD SEE ME-**
IT WOULD IGNITE IN THE HOLY PRESENCE OF **THE LIVING GOD ALMIGHTY.**

IF THE GATES OF SWEET **HEAVEN COULD SEE ME-** THEY WOULD KNOW THAT I NOW DANCE WITH THE HOLY ESSENCE AND **SPIRIT OF GOD ALMIGHTY.**

IF SWEET HEAVEN **COULD SEE ME-** IT WOULD BEHOLD THE BLESSED **MESSENGER OF GOD ALMIGHTY.**

IF SWEET HEAVEN COULD SEE-
IF SWEET HEAVEN COULD SEE-
IF SWEET HEAVEN COULD SEE-
IT WOULD BE A WITNESS TO THE ETERNAL PRESENCE OF **THE HOLY TRINITY AND BLESSED ME.**

HOLY, HOLY, HOLY-
IS THE BLESSED TRINITY CALLED GOD ALMIGHTY!!!

LISTEN TO MY HOLY SPIRIT WITHIN YOU, DEAR BARBARA

ALMIGHTY GOD SPEAKING TO BARBARA

LISTEN TO MY HOLY SPIRIT WITHIN YOU, **DEAR BARBARA.**

LISTEN TO THE SACRED VOICE AND SPIRIT OF **ALMIGHTY GOD, YOUR LOVING HEAVENLY FATHER.**

LISTEN. LISTEN. LISTEN.
RECEIVE ME, **O WORTHY DAUGHTER.**

DELIVER MY HOLY WORDS, **DEAR BARBARA-**
DELIVER THEM TO MY WORTHY SEARCHING **SON AND DAUGHTER.**

FOR, **HOLY AND TRUE-**
ARE THE WORDS THAT ARE **GIVEN TO YOU.**

ALLELUIA-
TO OUR HEAVENLY GOD AND **FATHER, JEHOVAH!!!**

SPEAK TO THEM, DEAR BARBARA, FOR THEY WILL **LISTEN TO ME.**
THEY WILL LISTEN TO THE INNER SPIRIT OF **CHRIST JESUS, THE ALMIGHTY.**

THEY WILL SEE-
THAT YOU CARRY THE FLESHLY BODY OF **CHRIST JESUS, THE ALMIGHTY.**

HOLY, HOLY, HOLY-
IS THE SACRED VOICE OF CHRIST ALMIGHTY!!!

HOLY, HOLY, HOLY-
IS THE VOICE AND SPIRIT OF GOD ALMIGHTY!!!

SPEAK TO THEM, **DEAR BARBARA.**
REVEAL MY HOLY ESSENCE TO MY SEARCHING **SON
AND DAUGHTER.**

WHEN YOU HEAR AND **FEEL ME, DEAR BARBARA-**
THEY WILL HEAR AND FEEL THE TRUE SPIRIT OF
GOD, THEIR HEAVENLY FATHER.

THEY WILL FEEL **MY DIVINE PRESENCE-**
AS YOU PROCLAIM **MY TRUE EXISTENCE.**

THEY WILL SEE-
THAT YOUR PURIFIED BODY CARRIES THE HOLY
ESSENCE OF **THE FOREVER-LIVING CHRIST JESUS,
THE ALMIGHTY.**

I WILL **SPEAK MY TRUTH-**
THAT WAS PRESENT **IN YOUR YOUTH.**

HOLY, HOLY, HOLY-
IS THE LORD GOD ALMIGHTY!!!

HALLELUJAH-
TO ALMIGHTY GOD JEHOVAH!!!

BARBARA AND SOME OF HER 61 GOD INSPIRED PUBLISHED BOOKS

SOME OF MY OTHER PUBLISHED BOOKS

1. WORDS OF INSPIRATION
2. FATHER, ARE YOU CALLING ME? (CHILDREN'S BOOK)
3. DAUGHTER OF COURAGE
4. A HOUSE DIVIDED CANNOT STAND
5. TASTE AND SEE THE GOODNESS OF THE LORD
6. HUMILITY- THE COST OF DISCIPLESHIP
7. WILL YOU BE MY BRIDE FIRST?
8. ODE TO MY BELOVED
9. FATHER, THEY KNOW NOT WHAT THEY DO
10. IN MY FATHER'S HOUSE (CHILDREN'S BOOK)
11. IN MY GARDEN (CHILDREN'S BOOK)
12. THE BATTLE IS OVER
13. THE GOSPEL ACCORDING TO THE LAMB'S BRIDE
14. THE PRESENT TESTAMENT
15. THE PRESENT TESTAMENT VOL. 2
16. THE PRESENT TESTAMENT VOL. 3
17. THE PRESENT TESTAMENT VOL. 4
18. THE PRESENT TESTAMENT VOL. 5
19. THE PRESENT TESTAMENT VOL. 6
20. THE PRESENT TESTAMENT VOL. 7

21. THE PRESENT TESTAMENT VOL. 8

22. THE PRESENT TESTAMENT VOL. 9

23. THE PRESENT TESTAMENT VOL. 10

24. THE PRESENT TESTAMENT VOL. 11

25. THE PRESENT TESTAMENT VOL. 12

26. THE PRESENT TESTAMENT VOL. 13

27. THE PRESENT TESTAMENT VOL. 14

28. THE PRESENT TESTAMENT VOL. 15

29. THE PRESENT TESTAMENT VOL. 16

30. THE PRESENT TESTAMENT VOL. 17

31. BEHOLD THE PRESENT TESTAMENT "VOLUMES 18, 19, 20, 21, 22 AND 23"

32. BEHOLD MY PRESENT TESTAMENT "VOLUMES 24 AND 25"

33. BEHOLD MY PRESENT TESTAMENT "VOLUMES 26, 27, 28 AND 29"

34. BEHOLD MY PRESENT TESTAMENT "VOLUMES 30, 31 AND 32"

35. BEHOLD MY PRESENT TESTAMENT "VOLUMES 33 AND 34"

36. BEHOLD MY PRESENT TESTAMENT "VOLUMES 35, 36 AND 37"

37. BEHOLD MY PRESENT TESTAMENT "VOLUMES 38 & 39"

38. BEHOLD MY PRESENT TESTAMENT "VOLUMES 40 & 41"

ALLYSON AND AUNTIE ENJOY GOD'S HOLY WORDS TODAY

Printed in the United States
by Baker & Taylor Publisher Services